Prayers of a Teen Poet

Poems and Illustrations

By

Sepi Shokuhi

Copyright © 2016 Sepi Shokuhi

All rights reserved.

ISBN: 069277999X
ISBN-13: 9780692779996
Library of Congress Control Number: 2016917589
Sepi shokuhi, Nashville, Tennessee

Scripture quotations marked (NIV) are taken from the Holy Bible, New International Version®, NIV®. Copyright © 1973, 1978, 1984, 2011 by Biblica, Inc.™ Used by permission of Zondervan. All rights reserved worldwide. www.zondervan.com The "NIV" and "New International Version" are trademarks registered in the United States Patent and Trademark Office by Biblica, Inc.™ - See more at: http://www.stevelaube.com/quote-the-bible-carefully/#sthash.mZ9J2BkX.dpuf

Acknowledgments

I would like to express my gratitude to friends, family, and loving pets who were great inspirations for my poems and illustrations and to all those who offered comments and support.

I would like to thank Mike Canterbury and Catherine Canterbury Groves for helping me with the review and selection of the Bible quotations.

Thanks to Jaime Branch, Teresa Thompson and Gina Kavanaugh for reviewing and editing the poems.

Last but not least, I would like to thank Jutta Ruck who encouraged me to publish this work.

To Maman, Rommi, Baby, and Lissa

Loving Pets

LOVE YOU, I whisper every day

Cheerfully into my cats' ears

Finding a way deep into their soul

The message is delivered to my peers

Pets don't speak our tongue

Yet, surely they know what it bears

Litter box clean enough, precious Molly?

Up to a walk, buddy Bear?

Attentive to their needs, I reach out

Beyond the boundary of plain duty

Where life uplifts to a higher realm

There I find no beast and no man

But pure love, rich and plenty

But the greatest of these is love.

(1 Corinthians 13:13) (NIV).

PEACE OF MIND

Praying is like speaking to the Lord

When praying, I am fair spoken

Even when troubles ambush me in the dark

And leave me little poise to afford

Or when restless thoughts like a tornado

Touch down with a blast of horror

I remind myself that divine peace

Will defeat their zombie-like roar

Imagine a spaceship led by God

And we the voyagers on board

Aiming for the remotest galaxies

Light-years in a blink of an eye

Are traveled by a gentle word

Submit to God and be at peace with him.

(Job 22:21) (NIV).

Delightfully Generous

Giving precedes receiving

Let's be generous givers

Let's volunteer for household chores

This time without making a fuss

You'll never know

Blessings flow unexpectedly

They are meant to surprise us

Then help a friend in need

This time with good grace

Bring out the angel inside you

Forget not the smile on your face

Giving gifts is another delight

When given without worry of lack

And guess what?

The goodness will return back

♥

The vivid faith to the One above

Is found within a gift

Carefully wrapped with love

Take delight in the LORD, and he will give you the desires of your heart.

(Psalm 37:4)(NIV).

Green Planet

Golden locks of harvest grain

Sway in an August afternoon

Untamed prairies dance for rain

Stately sequoias kiss the moon

From an island call the palm trees:

"Rest beneath our shades, eat our dates"

And sturdy remains the arctic willow

When the Nordic summer rapidly fades

A blue marble is our planet to space

Of life within, green is the color

Endowed upon us, the happy dwellers

From our worthy Maker whom we honor

You are worthy, our Lord and God, to receive glory and honor and power, for you created all things, and by your will they were created and have their being.

(Revelation 4:11)(NIV)

Send Forth Prayers

My prayers are as mighty as a falcon

Keen-eyed bird, swift in flight

One token from me and off it takes

The horizon reflecting on its eyes bright

Savage deserts and mountains it endures

Nothing takes down its divine height

My prayers are as gentle as butterflies,

Enchanting in the eye of the Beholder

Frivolously they flutter from bush to flower

Will they ever come back? I wonder

"Only God knows when," they respond

And keep dancing around the lavender

So is my word that goes out from my mouth: It will not return to me empty, but will accomplish what I desire and achieve the purpose for which I sent it.

(Isaiah 55:11)(NIV).

LET GO WITH LOVE

I let go without fear

♥

When sandcastles are taken by waves

Visions of washed-away dreams appear

Yet, higher truth is found beyond the waves

Where ocean brings me greater cheer

I let go without defeat

♥

A rocky road took me to a dead end

And grumbled:

"Mea culpa, I bruised your feet

Remember me as a gift of wisdom

And forget the misery of this retreat"

I let go with love

♥

Someone whom I loved with all my soul

Left my heart with a deep dark hole

Joy will be restored by the One above

So I let go my loved one…with love

Cast all your anxiety on him because he cares for you.

(1 Peter 5–7)(NIV).

Resurrection of Happiness

This frosty soil seeded a purpose

First showered in the tears I wept

Then nurtured by my praying voice

In the landscape of cold season

I sought for long

And looked in vain

To find that secret and its reason

Like searching for a lost child

Who never ran away

Just hidden

With mischief smitten

Under the veil of the winter's bride

The reign of frost had come to pass

But this was not the end

March arrived suddenly and

Banished it with an Easter Mass

A primrose caught my weary eyes

And woke me up from my winter blues

Without the words, it sang the truth:

"Faithful hearts will never lose"

But those who hope in the LORD will renew their strength.

(Isaiah 40:31)(NIV).

Bedtime Prayers

Dear God

In the solitude of night I seek thy presence

Before drifting into a current of dreams

I take a breath from thy holy essence

Praise and thanks for the given day

I whisper with a voice of a child

As if time had stopped to decay

From the first prayer taught by Mom

Once upon a time on Half Moon Bay

Words that filled my heart with glee

I'll teach them to my kids someday

In peace I will lie down and sleep, for you alone, LORD, make me dwell in safety.

(Psalms 4:8)(NIV).

True Love

If the sweet breeze of true love

Ever blows into my faithful heart

How do I know if it lasts for long?

Like in some old-fashioned song

Will it ravish emotions, eternally in prime?

Delighting a humble poem's rhyme?

Will it be the one and the only?

When times turn harsh and stormy?

Lord, one more thing I wish I knew

Will it draw me closer to you?

Love is patient, love is kind.

(1 Corinthians 13:4)(NIV).

Hope

"Hope is the thing with feathers"

Once wrote Emily Dickinson

May the God of hope fill you with joy

To merrily twitter at all weathers

Amen

I RATHER MERRILY QUACK

May the God of hope fill you with all joy and peace as you trust in him, so that you may overflow with hope by the power of the Holy Spirit.

(Romans 15:13)(NIV).